THE
Bon Appétit
KITCHEN
COLLECTION

Favorite
Cookies

The Knapp Press
Publishers

Los Angeles

Published by The Knapp Press
5900 Wilshire Boulevard, Los Angeles,
California 90036

Library of Congress Cataloging in Publication
Data
Main entry under title:

Favorite cookies.

(The Bon appétit kitchen collection)
Includes index.
1. Cookies. I. Title.
TX722.F376 1983   641.8'654   83-13622
ISBN 0-89535-123-4

Printed and bound in the United States of
America

On the cover: *Nougatine Rolls, Viennese
Sandwich Cookies, Grasshopper Bars, Sara's
Swedish Gem Cookies, Rosie's Mandelbrodt,
Petit Mont Blanc, Tuiles with Almonds*

Photograph by Dan Wolfe

Contents

1

Drop Cookies

Walnut Butter Cookies

Makes about 2½ dozen

- 1 cup all purpose flour
- ½ cup cornstarch
- ½ cup powdered sugar
- ¾ cup (1½ sticks) butter, room temperature
- ½ cup coarsely chopped or sliced walnuts

Preheat oven to 300°F. Sift first 3 ingredients into large bowl. Add butter and mix well. Stir in walnuts. Drop by rounded teaspoonfuls onto baking sheet. Bake until cookies are light golden, about 20 to 25 minutes.

Eggless Drop Cookies

Makes about 5 dozen

- ½ cup raw or firmly packed brown sugar
- ½ cup plus 2 tablespoons oil
- ⅓ cup honey

- 1 cup whole wheat flour
- ½ cup unbleached all purpose flour
- ½ cup soya flour
- 1 cup raisins
- ½ cup chopped nuts
- 2 teaspoons baking powder
- 1 teaspoon cinnamon
- ½ teaspoon salt
- ¼ teaspoon freshly grated nutmeg

Preheat oven to 375°F. Lightly grease baking sheet. Mix together sugar, oil and honey.

In separate large bowl, combine remaining ingredients. Add to sugar mixture and blend well. Pinch off about 1 tablespoon dough, flattening slightly, and drop on baking sheet (they spread very little). Bake 8 to 10 minutes or until browned.

Chocolate Drop Cookies

Makes 3 dozen

> 2 4-ounce bars German sweet chocolate
> 1 tablespoon unsalted butter
>
> 2 eggs
> ¾ cup sugar
> ¾ cup chopped pecans
> ¼ cup unbleached all purpose flour
> ½ teaspoon vanilla
> ¼ teaspoon baking powder
> ¼ teaspoon cinnamon
>   Pinch of salt

Preheat oven to 350°F. Grease baking sheets. Melt chocolate and butter in top of double boiler over simmering water. Set aside to cool.

Beat eggs in large bowl of electric mixer until foamy. Add sugar one teaspoon at a time and beat until thick, about 5 minutes. Blend in chocolate mixture, pecans, flour, vanilla, baking powder, cinnamon and salt and mix well. Drop dough by tablespoonfuls onto prepared baking sheets, spacing 2 inches apart. Bake 8 to 10 minutes. Let cool on baking sheets several minutes to prevent breaking before transferring to wire rack to cool completely. *Store cookies in airtight container.*

Luscious Lunch-Box Cookies

Makes about 7½ dozen

> 2 cups unbleached all purpose flour
> 1 teaspoon baking soda
> 1 teaspoon cinnamon
> ½ teaspoon baking powder
> ½ teaspoon salt
> 1 cup (2 sticks) unsalted butter
> 1 cup sugar
> 1 cup firmly packed light brown sugar
> 2 eggs
> 1 teaspoon vanilla
> 1 cup quick-cooking oats
> 1 cup crisp rice cereal

Preheat oven to 350°F. Sift flour, soda, cinnamon, baking powder and salt into bowl. Cream butter with sugars in another large bowl until light and fluffy. Stir in eggs and vanilla. Gradually blend in flour mixture, beating until smooth. Fold in oats and rice cereal. Drop by tablespoonfuls onto ungreased baking sheet. Bake until golden, about 10 to 12 minutes. Cool on wire rack. *Store in airtight container.*

Australian Brandy Snaps

Makes about 2½ dozen

- ½ cup (1 stick) butter
- ½ cup dark corn syrup
- ¼ cup firmly packed brown sugar
- ¾ cup all purpose flour

- 2 cups whipping cream
- ½ cup sugar
- 2 tablespoons brandy

Preheat oven to 375°F. Generously grease both baking sheet and handle of wooden spoon. Combine butter, syrup and brown sugar in small saucepan. Place over medium heat and stir until butter melts. Mix in flour. Bring to boil, stirring constantly. Remove from heat and let stand until slightly thickened but still warm. *Mixture must not cool; place pan in another pan of water (110°F to 120°F) to maintain proper consistency.*

Drop batter by scant teaspoonfuls onto baking sheet, making no more than 5 per batch, as snaps harden quickly and must be rolled very quickly after removal from oven. Bake 4 to 5 minutes, until bubbly and golden. Let cool only slightly. *Working quickly,* roll up on handle of wooden spoon, forming cylinders about ¾ to 1 inch in diameter. Remove and transfer to rack to cool. *If cookies become too firm to roll, return sheet to oven about 1 to 2 minutes to soften.*

Lightly whip cream. Gradually add sugar and continue beating until stiff. Quickly blend in brandy. Spoon into pastry bag fitted with plain tip. Pipe into each cookie, filling from each end into middle. Serve immediately. *Store unfilled cookies in airtight container.*

Carob Chip Cookies

Makes 3 dozen

- ½ cup (1 stick) butter
- ¾ cup firmly packed brown sugar
- 2 eggs, beaten
- 2 teaspoons vanilla
- ¾ cup whole wheat pastry flour
- ⅓ cup raw wheat germ
- ¼ cup unbleached all purpose flour
- ½ cup powdered milk
- 2 teaspoons baking powder
- ½ teaspoon salt
- 1 6-ounce package carob chips
- ½ cup chopped nuts

Preheat oven to 375°F. Grease baking sheet. Cream together butter and sugar. Beat in eggs and vanilla. Mix together pastry flour, wheat germ, unbleached flour, milk, baking powder and salt, and add to moist ingredients. Blend in carob chips and chopped nuts.

Drop by teaspoonfuls on baking sheet and bake 8 to 10 minutes, until cookies are lightly golden.

Big Deals

Makes 3 dozen large cookies

- 1 cup (2 sticks) butter
- ¾ cup firmly packed brown sugar
- ½ cup raw unfiltered honey
- 2 eggs, lightly beaten
- 2 teaspoons vanilla

- 1⅓ cups unbleached all purpose flour
- 1 teaspoon sea salt
- 1 teaspoon baking soda
- 3 cups old-fashioned rolled oats
- 1 cup raisins
- ½ cup pumpkin seeds
- ½ cup sunflower seeds
- ½ cup raw wheat germ

Preheat oven to 375°F. Cream butter, brown sugar and honey until light and creamy. Add eggs and vanilla and beat thoroughly.

Sift together flour, salt and baking soda. Add gradually to butter mixture. Add oats, raisins, pumpkin seeds, sunflower seeds and wheat germ. Blend well.

Drop heaping tablespoonfuls of batter 3½ to 4 inches apart on lightly oiled baking sheet. Bake until golden brown, about 10 to 12 minutes.

Dentelles

Makes 12 to 16

- ½ cup powdered sugar
- ½ cup (1 stick) butter, cut into small pieces
- ⅓ cup light corn syrup
- ½ cup all purpose flour
- 1½ tablespoons anise liqueur or Galliano
- 1 tablespoon anise seed

Preheat oven to 350°F. Generously butter 2 baking sheets and set aside. Combine sugar, butter and corn syrup in small saucepan. Place over low heat and cook, stirring several times, until butter is melted; *do not boil.* Remove from heat. Add flour and beat until smooth with whisk or electric mixer. Stir in liqueur and anise seed. *Mixture will be thin but will thicken as it stands.*

Spoon batter for 2 cookies on each baking sheet, using 1 tablespoon for each (they will spread considerably). Bake 8 to

10 minutes, until cookies are golden and have *almost* stopped bubbling. Cool 1½ to 2 minutes on sheet; *do not remove sooner or cookies will flatten and collapse.* Carefully remove with large metal spatula and slide onto paper towels, folding cookie loosely into fan shape. There should be enough butter left on baking sheets so cookies can be removed easily, but brush or rub lightly between bakings to distribute evenly.

Dentelles can also be loosely rolled into thirds or formed into cup shapes.

Tuiles with Almonds

Makes 2 dozen

- ½ cup sugar
  Dash of vanilla
- ⅓ cup egg whites (about 2 to 4)

- ⅓ cup all purpose flour
- ¼ cup melted clarified butter

½ cup ground almonds
1 tablespoon grated orange rind

½ cup slivered almonds

Preheat oven to 325°F. Combine sugar, vanilla and egg whites in bowl. Beat until mixture is foamy, about 1 minute.

Add flour, butter, ground almonds and orange rind, mixing thoroughly.

Drop batter by teaspoonfuls on greased baking sheet, allowing no more than 8 cookies per baking. Sprinkle with slivered almonds. Bake about 8 to 10 minutes or until edges of cookies are brown. Remove one at a time and place immediately on a narrow rolling pin or over a bottle. Allow to cool completely on rolling pin. *Store in covered tin up to 1 week.*

If cookies harden before you are able to remove from baking sheet, return them to oven for a few moments to soften.

Nougatine Rolls

Makes 2 dozen

- ⅔ cup medium fine chopped almonds or filberts
- 2 tablespoons instant flour
- ¼ teaspoon salt
- ½ cup sugar
- ½ cup (1 stick) unsalted butter, room temperature
- 2 tablespoons whipping cream

Preheat oven to 375°F. Place nuts on baking sheet and toast 5 minutes, stirring several times to brown evenly.

Place all ingredients in a 2-quart saucepan. Mix thoroughly. Cook over low heat until mixture begins to bubble, about 5 minutes, stirring occasionally. Remove from heat and stir briskly about 30 seconds.

Spacing evenly, drop 4 teaspoonfuls of dough on greased baking sheet. Bake 4 to 6 minutes or until golden brown and batter has stopped bubbling. Remove from oven and allow to stand 1 minute. Remove with wide spatula.

Working quickly, place cookies one at a time over buttered wooden broom handle or dowel, roll snugly, then gently slip cookie off. Cool on cake rack.

Store in airtight container up to 2 weeks.

Peanut Butter Favorites

Makes 5 dozen

- ¾ cup peanut butter (preferably homemade)*
- ½ cup (1 stick) unsalted butter, room temperature
- 1¼ cups unbleached all purpose flour
- ½ cup sugar
- ½ cup firmly packed brown sugar
- 1 egg
- 1 teaspoon baking soda
- ¼ teaspoon baking powder
  Pinch of salt

*Natural food stores carry peanut butter with no added oil or salt that can be substituted for homemade.

Preheat oven to 350°F. Lightly grease baking sheets. Combine peanut butter and butter in large bowl. Add flour, sugars, egg, baking soda, baking powder and salt and mix well. Roll dough into 1-inch balls and arrange 3 inches apart on baking sheets. Press crisscross pattern on cookies using fork. Bake until golden, about 10 to 12 minutes. Transfer to wire rack and let cool. *Store in airtight container.*

Pumpkin Pistachio Macaroons

These are time-consuming but well worth the effort.

Makes 2 dozen

⅔ cup raw unfiltered honey

¼ cup chopped pumpkin seeds

¼ cup finely chopped unsalted, undyed pistachios

2 cups unsweetened
   shredded coconut (or
   more)
¼ teaspoon crushed anise
   seeds
3 egg whites, stiffly beaten

Preheat oven to 300°F. Blend honey, pumpkin seeds, pistachios, coconut and anise. Fold in egg whites. (Add more coconut if batter is too thin.) Drop by teaspoonfuls onto lightly oiled baking sheet. Bake 25 to 30 minutes or until golden brown.

Let cookies stand about 10 to 15 minutes before removing from sheet. They will be sticky and soft. Place in single layer on clean baking sheet or plates.

When all cookies are baked and oven has cooled to 100°F to 150°F, return cookies to oven to dry for at least 1 hour or overnight.

Glazed Apple Gems

Makes about 6 dozen

- ½ cup (1 stick) unsalted butter, room temperature
- 1⅓ cups firmly packed brown sugar
- 1 egg
- 1 large apple, peeled, cored and finely chopped
- 1 cup finely chopped raisins
- 1 cup finely chopped walnuts or filberts
- ¼ cup apple juice
- 1 teaspoon finely grated lemon peel
- 2 cups unbleached all purpose flour
- 1 teaspoon baking soda
- 1 teaspoon cinnamon
- 1 teaspoon freshly grated nutmeg

Glaze
- 1½ cups sifted powdered sugar
- 3 tablespoons apple or fresh lemon juice
- 1 tablespoon unsalted butter

Preheat oven to 375°F. Grease baking sheets. Cream butter with sugar in large bowl until light and fluffy. Stir in egg, apple, raisins, nuts, apple juice and lemon peel. Blend in flour, baking soda, cinnamon and nutmeg and mix well. Drop dough by tablespoonfuls onto prepared sheets. Bake 10 to 12 minutes.

Meanwhile, prepare glaze. Blend sugar, juice and butter in processor or blender. Transfer mixture to bowl.

Remove cookies from oven. Let cool slightly on wire rack. Dip top of each warm cookie into glaze, swirling to cover. Return to wire rack to allow excess glaze to drip through and cool completely. *Store glazed gems in airtight container.*

Raisin-Granola Cookies

Makes 4 to 5 dozen

- 1 cup (2 sticks) butter, room temperature
- ¾ cup firmly packed dark brown sugar
- ¾ cup sugar
- 1 egg
- 1 teaspoon vanilla
- 1½ cups all purpose flour
- 1 teaspoon baking soda
- 1 teaspoon salt
- 1¾ cups granola
- 1 cup seedless raisins
- ½ cup unsalted peanuts

Preheat oven to 375°F. Generously grease baking sheets. Cream together butter and sugars. Add egg and vanilla and continue beating until well blended. Sift together flour, baking soda and salt. Add in small amounts alternately with granola, beating well after each addition. Continue beating 2 to 3 minutes, until batter is very well blended. Stir in raisins and unsalted peanuts.

Drop batter by heaping teaspoonfuls about 2 inches apart

on prepared sheets. Bake until the cookies are lightly browned around edges but still soft, about 12 to 15 minutes. Loosen with spatula and cool on racks. *Store in airtight container.*

Cookies freeze well.

Orange Drop Cookies

A cakelike cookie that requires fresh, unstrained orange juice. Can be frozen after icing and travels well for picnics.

Makes about 3 dozen

- ⅔ cup unsalted butter, room temperature
- 1 cup sugar
- 2 eggs
- ½ cup freshly squeezed orange juice
- 1 tablespoon freshly grated orange peel
- 2¼ cups unbleached all purpose flour
- ½ teaspoon salt

½ teaspoon baking soda
½ cup coarsely chopped walnuts

Icing
1½ cups sifted powdered sugar
3 tablespoons butter, room temperature
1½ tablespoons freshly squeezed orange juice
2 teaspoons freshly grated orange peel

Preheat oven to 350°F. Generously grease baking sheets. Cream butter with sugar in large bowl until light and fluffy. Stir in eggs, orange juice and peel. Add flour, salt and baking soda and mix well. Fold in nuts. Drop dough by large tablespoonfuls onto prepared baking sheets. Bake until golden brown, about 10 minutes. Cool on rack.

For icing, blend all ingredients in medium bowl until smooth. Swirl icing over tops of cookies, covering completely. *Store in airtight container.*

2

Refrigerator and Specialty Cookies

Painted Sugar Cookies

These colorful cookies may be baked and frozen; let them stand at room temperature to thaw.

Makes about 3 dozen

    1 cup (2 sticks) butter or margarine, or mixture of both
  1½ cups powdered sugar
    1 egg
    1 teaspoon vanilla
    ½ teaspoon almond extract

2½ cups all purpose flour
1 teaspoon baking soda
1 teaspoon cream of tartar

1 small can (4 ounces)
 evaporated milk
 Liquid or paste food
 coloring
 All purpose flour

Cream butter or margarine in medium bowl with electric mixer. Add sugar and beat well. Thoroughly blend in egg, then add vanilla and almond extract.

Mix together flour, baking soda and cream of tartar in separate small bowl, then beat into creamed butter mixture and blend well. Form this dough into a ball and wrap in plastic wrap. Chill in refrigerator about 3 hours so dough will be firm enough to roll easily.

Lightly grease several baking sheets. Gather 1 or 2 small, very clean paintbrushes, and make cookie paint as follows: Pour 1 tablespoon evaporated milk into each of several small bowls or into sections of a muffin tin. Tint each with a different color of liquid or paste food coloring (paste will give a more vibrant color).

Preheat oven to 375°F. Arrange some cooling racks on counter. Divide chilled dough into thirds and work with 1 section at a time. Leave remainder wrapped in refrigerator. Lightly flour counter or board and flour rolling pin. Roll out dough about ¼ inch thick, then cut into shapes with cookie cutters.

Using a spatula or metal pancake turner, carefully lift cookies and place on prepared baking sheets. Using brush, paint bright designs on unbaked cookies with milk and food coloring mixtures. If possible, place baking sheets in refrigerator for a few minutes before baking.

Bake in preheated oven about 7 to 8 minutes or until cookies are very lightly browned. Transfer baked cookies to cooling racks to crisp; let cool completely.

Store cookies in a tin or plastic box with waxed paper between layers for protection.

A few hints: It is easier to pre-pare a whole baking sheet of cookies before starting to paint.

Use one color on all cookies be-fore painting with the next color (you may use more than one color on each cookie).

After all cookies have been cut from a section of dough, place any scraps of dough in a single layer rather than in a ball. When all dough has been used, gently pat and pinch single layers of scraps into new sheets. Roll lightly to blend dough, then cut out more cookies.

Wedding Cookies

Buttery and rich, these be-loved Mexican sweets are thickly coated with powdered sugar while still warm. They can be made one day ahead.

Makes about 1 dozen

   ½ cup (1 stick) unsalted
      butter, room
      temperature
   1 cup all purpose flour

¼ cup sifted powdered sugar

½ cup finely chopped toasted pecans or almonds

½ teaspoon vanilla
  Pinch of salt

  Powdered sugar

Position rack in center of oven and preheat to 350°F. Beat butter until light and fluffy. Add flour, ¼ cup powdered sugar, nuts, vanilla and salt and continue beating until mixture forms soft dough. Wrap tightly and freeze 1 hour, or refrigerate (preferably overnight) until dough is firm enough to pinch off in pieces the size of large walnuts.

Roll pieces between palms of hands into balls or half-moon shapes. Space about 1½ inches apart on ungreased baking sheet. Bake until cookies are pale golden, about 20 minutes. Cool slightly on wire racks. Dust generously with powdered sugar while still warm.

Viennese Sandwich Cookies

Makes 3 dozen

- 1 cup (2 sticks) unsalted butter, room temperature
- 1 cup sugar
- 1 egg yolk
- 1 teaspoon vanilla
- 2 cups all purpose flour

  Sugar

- 2 cups powdered sugar
- ½ cup (1 stick) unsalted butter, room temperature
  2 to 4 tablespoons fresh lemon juice

- 2 ounces semisweet chocolate
- 1 tablespoon butter

  Chopped nuts, varicolored nonpareils or shredded coconut (garnish)

Cream together butter and sugar. Add egg yolk, vanilla and flour, mixing thoroughly. Chill at least 2 hours.

Make 72 balls of dough the size of small walnuts. Place 2 inches apart on ungreased cookie sheets. Preheat oven to 325°F. Dip bottom of small glass into sugar and use it to flatten each ball to a thickness of ⅛ inch. Bake 10 to 12 minutes until cookies are lightly colored with slight brown edges. *Do not overbake.* Place on cooling rack.

Cream powdered sugar and butter. Add lemon juice to taste (it should be tart). Spread a teaspoonful of mixture on half the baked cookies. Cover each one with another cookie, making a sandwich.

In double boiler heat chocolate and butter until just melted. Dip an edge of each cookie sandwich into chocolate, then into nuts, nonpareils or coconut. Place on cooling rack to set.

Store in tightly covered container, layered with sheets of waxed paper, or freeze.

Espresso Nut Cookies

Makes about 2 dozen

- 1 tablespoon instant espresso powder
- 1 tablespoon hot water

- 2 cups all purpose flour
- 1 teaspoon baking powder
- ⅛ teaspoon salt
- ½ cup (1 stick) butter, room temperature
- 1 cup sugar
- 1 egg
- ½ cup finely chopped walnuts

Dissolve espresso powder in hot water; cool. Set aside.

Sift flour, baking powder and salt. Cream butter in large bowl. Gradually add sugar, beating until fluffy. Add egg and cooled espresso and beat well. Blend in flour mixture; stir in nuts. Divide dough in half and shape into 2-inch cylinders. Wrap in waxed paper and chill (or wrap in foil and freeze).

When ready to bake, preheat oven to 375°F. Grease baking sheets. Slice cylinders into ¼-inch rounds and arrange on prepared sheets. Bake until firm and lightly browned, about 8 to 10 minutes. Transfer cookies to racks and let cool. *Store in airtight container.*

Marshmallow Mosaics

Makes 6 rolls

> 6 ounces semisweet chocolate
>
> 2 eggs
> 1 teaspoon vanilla
> 1 10½-ounce bag colored miniature marshmallows
> 1½ cups finely chopped toasted nuts
>
> 2 cups graham cracker crumbs

Melt chocolate in top of double boiler, stirring occasionally.

Remove top pan from heat; beat in eggs and vanilla. Fold in marshmallows and 1 cup nuts.

Combine remaining nuts and graham cracker crumbs.

Cut 6 pieces of waxed paper 12 inches long. Spread crumb mixture evenly over half of each piece of waxed paper, keeping crumb side closest to you. Place spoonfuls of the marshmallow-chocolate mixture along edge of waxed paper atop crumbs, dividing the mixture among the 6 pieces. Using waxed paper as a roller, carefully shape each mosaic into a roll 1½ to 2 inches thick. Twist ends of waxed paper and refrigerate until chocolate has hardened.

With serrated knife, cut on diagonal into ¼-inch slices.

Rolls may be wrapped in foil and stored in freezer indefinitely for slicing as needed.

Leaf Cookies

Makes about 4 dozen

- 1 cup (2 sticks) butter, softened
- ⅓ cup sugar (preferably superfine)
- 6 ounces finely ground almonds (1½ cups firmly packed)
- 1 cup all purpose flour
- 1 teaspoon vanilla

½ teaspoon almond extract

Metal leaf stencil*

6 ounces semisweet
chocolate (or more), cut
into 1-inch pieces

Preheat oven to 375°F. Cream
butter and sugar until light and
fluffy. Add almonds, flour, vanilla and almond extract and
mix until smooth.

Place leaf stencil on ungreased
baking sheet and press dough
into design with spatula. (If
room is warm, you may need to
chill dough briefly before apply-
ing stencil.) Wipe off excess
dough and gently lift stencil off
so cookie adheres to sheet. Repeat until all dough is used,
leaving 1½ inches between
cookies. Bake 6 to 7 minutes or
until edges are golden brown.
Cool on baking sheet 1 to 3 minutes, then carefully remove to
wire racks and cool completely.

Soften chocolate in top of double boiler over hot, but not boiling, water. Carefully spread on

*Single or double leaf stencils are available
in cookware shops or department stores.

bottom of leaves, marking off veins with edge of knife or spatula, or assemble pastry bag and pipe from smallest plain tube for three-dimensional look. Allow to set in cool area (60°F to 65°F) until firm. *Store cookies in airtight container between sheets of waxed paper.*

Buttery Nut Balls

Makes about 3 dozen

>   1 cup black walnuts
> ¼ cup sunflower seeds
> ¼ cup chia or sesame
>   seeds
> ¼ cup tahini (sesame
>   butter)
> ¼ cup raw unfiltered honey
> ¼ cup crunchy natural
>   peanut butter
>   1 cup carob chips

Grind black walnuts, sunflower seeds and sesame seeds in processor or blender. Turn mixture into bowl and add tahini, honey and peanut butter. Blend well.

Form into small balls, rolling each in carob chips. Chill in single layer.

May be stored in tightly covered container for a week or more.

First Dates

Makes about 3 dozen

> 1 cup sugar
> 2 eggs
> ½ cup unbleached all purpose flour
> ½ teaspoon baking powder
> ¼ teaspoon salt
> 1 cup whole dates, pitted and chopped
> 1 cup chopped pecans or walnuts
> ¼ cup sugar

Preheat oven to 350°F. Generously grease 8-inch glass baking dish. Beat 1 cup sugar and eggs in large bowl until fluffy. Sift flour, baking powder and salt into sugar mixture and blend well. Fold in dates and nuts. Turn into prepared pan. Bake *exactly* 30 minutes. Remove from oven *immediately* and stir, mixing well. Cool completely. Shape into bite-size balls. Roll in remaining sugar. *Store in airtight container.*

Rosie's Mandelbrodt

Makes approximately 6 dozen

- 1 cup (2 sticks) butter
- 2 cups sugar
- 6 eggs

- 4½ cups all purpose flour
- 1 tablespoon baking powder
- 1 teaspoon almond extract
- 2 2⅓-ounce jars chocolate sprinkles
- 2 cups chopped toasted almonds

Preheat oven to 350°F. Cream butter and sugar. Add eggs one at a time, beating mixture well after each addition.

Add flour, baking powder and almond extract. Mix well. Fold in chocolate sprinkles and almonds. Place into four oiled 9 × 5-inch pans; dough should be ¾ inch deep. Bake 20 to 25 minutes or until dry.

Turn out onto cutting board. While still warm, use a serrated knife to cut each loaf into ⅜- to ½-inch slices. Place slices on baking sheet. Toast 5 to 10 minutes on each side, or until lightly browned.

Store in tightly covered container or freeze.

Mandelbrodt with Chocolate Chips

Makes about 3 dozen

3 cups all purpose flour
2 teaspoons baking powder
½ teaspoon salt
1 cup plus 1 tablespoon vegetable oil
1 cup sugar
3 eggs
1 cup finely chopped pecans
4 ounces chocolate chips

5 tablespoons sugar
1 tablespoon cinnamon

Preheat oven to 375°F. Grease 2 baking sheets. Mix flour, baking powder and salt in medium bowl. Set aside. Beat oil, 1 cup sugar and eggs in large bowl. Gradually add 2 cups flour mixture, beating constantly. Fold in pecans and chocolate chips. Add remaining flour mixture and mix well.

Lightly flour hands. Divide dough into fourths. Transfer to baking sheets. Shape into flat loaves about 3 inches wide and about ¾ inch high. Combine remaining sugar and cinnamon in small bowl and sprinkle evenly over each. Bake 20 minutes. Cut each loaf into ½-inch slices. Turn slices cut side up and continue baking until toasted and golden, about 15 minutes. Cool completely. *Store Mandelbrodt in airtight containers.*

Mandelbrodt freezes well.

Deep-Fried Wafer Cookies (Galettes de Noël)

Makes about 20 to 30

  4 cups all purpose flour
  2 tablespoons sugar
  1 teaspoon baking powder
  1 teaspoon salt
  2 large eggs, well beaten
  ¾ cup milk
  1 tablespoon orange flower water*
   Grated peel of 1 lemon
  ¼ cup (½ stick) butter, melted

   Oil for deep frying
   Powdered sugar

   Honey (optional)

Sift flour, sugar, baking powder and salt into large bowl. In separate bowl, combine well-beaten eggs, milk, orange flower water and lemon peel. Add to dry ingredients. Stir in butter, then mix well with hands until smooth, workable, not too sticky dough is formed. If dough is difficult to

*Available in specialty food sections of markets and in some liquor stores.

handle, add a little more flour or milk as needed, until it is a workable consistency.

Form dough into 20 to 30 small balls about the size of large walnuts, then let stand covered with cloth about 25 minutes.

Heat oil in deep, heavy pot or fryer to 370°F to 375°F. Flatten each ball of dough into circle about 6 inches across and ⅛ inch thick. Fry a few at a time in hot oil, turning once, until lightly browned on both sides. Drain on paper towels, dip in powdered sugar and pile on serving platter. Continue until all dough is fried.

If desired, heat honey and place in small bowl for dipping. Serve galettes while still warm.

3

Filled Cookies

Sara's Swedish Gem Cookies

Makes 3 dozen

- 1 cup (2 sticks) unsalted butter
- ½ cup sugar
- 2 cups all purpose flour
- 2 egg yolks

- 2 egg whites
- 1½ to 2 cups chopped nuts

- 1 11-ounce jar raspberry jam

Cream butter and sugar. Add flour and egg yolks and beat 1 minute. Chill.

Make 36 balls of dough the size of small walnuts. Dip balls into slightly beaten egg white, then roll in chopped nuts. Place 1½ inches apart on greased cookie sheet, allowing room for cookies to spread.

Preheat oven to 325°F. Flatten balls to a thickness of ¼ inch with bottom of a small glass. Using a thimble or fingertip, make a slight indentation in center of each cookie. Fill with jam. Bake until lightly browned, about 12 to 15 minutes.

Store in tightly covered container, layered with sheets of waxed paper, or freeze.

Linzer Cookies

Makes about 2 dozen

- 1¼ cups whole wheat pastry flour
- 2 teaspoons cinnamon
- ½ teaspoon freshly grated nutmeg
- ¼ teaspoon ground cardamom
- ¼ cup (½ stick) unsalted butter

2 small egg yolks
2 tablespoons light honey
1 teaspoon vanilla

¼ cup Raspberry Jam
   Syrup (see following
   recipe)

Combine flour, cinnamon, nutmeg and cardamom in processor and mix well. Add butter and
blend, using on/off turns, until
mixture resembles coarse meal.
Combine egg yolks, honey and
vanilla in small bowl. Add to
flour mixture and blend until
combined but crumbly. Gather
into ball.

Preheat oven to 350°F. Roll dough
out between 2 sheets of floured
waxed paper to thickness of ³/₁₆
inch. Cut into rounds using 1½-
inch cookie cutter. Set half of
rounds aside. Cut centers out of
remaining rounds using ½-inch-
diameter plain pastry tip, forming rings. Repeat rolling and
cutting using excess pastry and
dough cut from centers.

Arrange dough rounds and rings
on baking sheet. Bake 15 minutes. Let cool. Spread rounds
with Raspberry Jam Syrup. Ar-

range rings on top. Chill until jam sets. *Store in airtight container in cool, dark place.*

Raspberry Jam Syrup

Use as a filling for Linzer Cookies or as a spread for toast or muffins.

Makes ¼ cup

- ¼ cup seedless honey-sweetened red or black raspberry jam
- 1 teaspoon fresh lemon juice

Combine jam and lemon juice in small saucepan over medium heat and stir until jam is melted. Let cool to room temperature before using.

Rugulah

Makes 4 dozen

Filling
    1 cup finely ground
       walnuts
    1 cup raisins or currants
    ½ cup sugar
    1 tablespoon cinnamon

Cookie Dough
  3½ cups (or more)
       unbleached all purpose
       flour
    1 cup sugar
    ⅔ cup unsalted butter,
       room temperature
    3 eggs
    2 tablespoons honey
    2 teaspoons baking
       powder
    ¼ teaspoon salt

    ½ cup (1 stick) butter,
       melted

For filling, combine walnuts, raisins or currants, sugar and cinnamon in small bowl and blend well. Set aside.

For dough, combine 3½ cups flour with sugar, butter, eggs, honey, baking powder and salt in large bowl, adding more flour as necessary to make pliable dough. Divide dough into thirds. Flatten into discs between sheets of waxed paper. Refrigerate at least 2 hours.

Preheat oven to 350°F. Grease and flour baking sheet, shaking off excess flour. Remove one batch of dough from refrigerator. Roll out into 12-inch circle. Brush generously with melted butter. Sprinkle with ⅓ cinnamon mixture; pat mixture into dough. Drizzle a little more butter over top. Cut into 16 wedges using pizza cutter or very sharp knife. Roll each triangle up from outside edge to point.

Arrange on prepared baking sheet point side down. Bake until golden, about 15 to 18 minutes, watching carefully to prevent burning. Let cool on wire rack. Repeat with remaining dough. *Store Rugulah in airtight container.*

Nut Cookies

Makes about 3 dozen

- 1 cup (2 sticks) butter, chilled and cut into pieces
- 2½ cups all purpose flour
- 4 to 5 tablespoons frozen orange juice concentrate, thawed

- 1 cup chopped pistachios, almonds or walnuts
- ¾ cup sugar
- 1 teaspoon cinnamon
- ¼ teaspoon ground cloves
  Vanilla-flavored powdered sugar*

Preheat oven to 350°F. Generously grease baking sheet. Cut butter into flour using pastry blender or knives. Add enough orange juice concentrate to make soft dough.

Combine nuts, sugar, cinnamon and cloves. Pinch off dough into walnut-size pieces. Roll each

*For vanilla-flavored powdered sugar, pour 1 pound powdered sugar into wide-necked 1-quart jar. Split vanilla bean lengthwise. Scrape seeds into sugar, placing empty pod on top. Cover and shake. Let stand several days before using, shaking occasionally.

into a ball, making an impression in center with your finger. Place about 1 teaspoonful nut mixture in hollow. Reroll into ball. Transfer to prepared baking sheet. Bake 20 minutes or until very lightly colored; *do not allow to brown.* Transfer to racks and cool completely. (Cookies will crisp as they cool.) Carefully roll in powdered sugar. *Store in airtight container.*

Sweet Crescents (Teem Gok)

Makes 5 to 6 dozen

- ½ cup chopped dried apricots*
- ½ cup chopped dark raisins*
- ½ cup chopped dates*
- ½ cup chopped salted peanuts*
- ½ cup flaked coconut
- ½ cup firmly packed brown sugar
- ½ cup sugar

*Other dried fruits and nuts, such as apples, prunes, sesame seeds, walnuts and almonds, may be used.

5 to 6 dozen won ton
  wrappers
3 to 4 cups vegetable oil

1 egg, lightly beaten

Combine first 7 ingredients and
mix well. Fold each won ton
wrapper diagonally and round
off top corners with scissors.
Heat oil in deep fryer to 375°F.

Open won tons and place about
1 teaspoon filling in center of
each. Moisten edges with beaten
egg and seal gently. Deep fry in
batches until golden, turning
once. Drain on paper towels and
set aside to cool. *Store in airtight container.*

*Excellent warm or cold as an ac-
companiment to ice cream.*

4

Bars and Squares

Slovenian Almond Squares

These crunchy cookies are similar to the familiar Italian *biscotti*.

Makes 20

- 1 cup all purpose flour
- ¾ cup ground almonds
- ¾ cup powdered sugar
- ½ cup (1 stick) butter, room temperature
- ¼ cup (2 ounces) egg whites
- 2 ounces unsweetened chocolate, grated
- 2 ounces semisweet chocolate, grated

1 egg, lightly beaten
20 blanched whole almonds

Preheat oven to 350°F. Generously grease 8-inch square baking pan. Combine first 7 ingredients in bowl and blend well. Turn into pan, spreading evenly to edges. Brush with beaten egg. Mark into squares and top each with an almond. Bake 35 to 40 minutes.

Apple Walnut Squares

Makes about 2 dozen

2 cups all purpose flour
2 cups firmly packed brown sugar
½ cup (1 stick) butter, room temperature
1 cup chopped walnuts
1 teaspoon cinnamon
1 teaspoon baking soda
¼ teaspoon salt
1 egg
1 cup sour cream
1 teaspoon vanilla
2 cups (about 2 large) finely chopped peeled tart apples

Vanilla ice cream

Preheat oven to 350°F. Lightly grease 9 × 13-inch baking dish.

Combine first 3 ingredients in medium bowl and mix until finely crumbled. Stir in nuts. Press 2 cups of mixture evenly into bottom of prepared dish. Add cinnamon, baking soda and salt to remaining mixture and blend well. Beat in egg, sour cream and vanilla. Gently stir in apples. Spoon evenly into dish. Bake until cake begins to pull away from sides of dish and tester inserted in center comes out clean, about 35 to 40 minutes. Let cool completely in pan. Cut into squares. Top with vanilla ice cream.

Apricot Prune Bars

Makes 40

- ½ cup (1 stick) unsalted butter
- 1 cup sugar
- 3 cups all purpose flour
- 1 tablespoon baking powder
- 2 eggs
- ¼ teaspoon salt

   1 12-ounce box pitted
       prunes
       Prune juice

  12 ounces dried apricots
       Apricot nectar

   2 cups shredded coconut
   1 cup chopped toasted
       walnuts

       Powdered sugar

Combine butter, sugar, flour, baking powder, eggs and salt. Mix thoroughly. Press half of dough into bottom of oiled 9 × 13 × 2-inch pan. Refrigerate. Shape remaining dough into a ball and freeze until firm.

Cover prunes with prune juice. Allow to set until prunes are plumped. Puree with juice in processor or blender.

Cover apricots with apricot nectar, bring to a simmer and gently poach until soft. Puree apricots with nectar.

Preheat oven to 350°F. Spread prune mixture over dough-lined pan. Cover with 1 cup coconut. Coarsely grate half the frozen dough over the coconut, distributing it evenly. Spoon the apricot puree over the grated dough; cover with nuts. Coarsely grate remaining dough over the nut layer; cover with remaining coconut. Bake for 60 to 70 minutes. Cool. Before cutting, place in freezer 1 hour. Cut, then dust with powdered sugar.

Store in tightly covered container or freeze.

Fig Squares

Makes 1 dozen large squares

Crust
    3 cups pastry flour
    1½ teaspoons sugar
    1½ teaspoons salt
    1 cup vegetable shortening
    7 to 9 tablespoons water

Filling
    1 pound finely chopped dried figs
    1¼ cups water
    1½ cups sugar
    4 teaspoons fresh lemon juice

    Milk

Sift together flour, sugar and salt. Cut in shortening with pastry blender. Add water as needed a little at a time until mixture holds together. Chill thoroughly.

While pastry is chilling, combine four filling ingredients thoroughly and simmer gently, stirring occasionally, until mixture is consistency of marmalade, about 15 minutes. Cool.

Preheat oven to 400°F. Divide chilled dough into 2 equal pieces. Roll out to a thickness of about ⅛ inch. Line 11½ × 8½ × ¾-inch pan with one sheet of dough, patting to fit evenly. Spread cooled filling over lower crust. Cover with remaining sheet of dough, seal edges and make steam vents in several places. Brush top crust with milk and bake 25 to 30 minutes, until pastry is golden brown. Cool before cutting into squares.

Squares freeze beautifully.

Oatmeal Raisin Bars

Makes about 7 dozen

- ¾ cup (1½ sticks) butter or margarine
- ⅔ cup honey
- 2 eggs
- 2 teaspoons vanilla
- 2½ cups old-fashioned rolled oats
- 1 cup whole wheat pastry flour
- ½ cup chopped nuts
- ½ cup raisins
- 2 teaspoons baking powder
- ½ teaspoon salt

Preheat oven to 325°F. Lightly grease 11 × 16-inch baking sheet with raised sides. Cream together butter or margarine, honey, eggs and vanilla. Add remaining ingredients and mix well. Spread evenly on baking sheet and bake 25 to 30 minutes. Cool and cut into squares.

Mixed Fruit Bars

Makes 16 2-inch squares

- 1½ cups unbleached or whole wheat pastry flour
- ⅓ cup raw wheat germ
- 2 teaspoons baking powder
- ½ teaspoon salt
- 1½ cups chopped mixed dried fruit (dates, prunes and apricots are best)
- ½ cup chopped walnuts
- 3 tablespoons sesame seeds

- 3 eggs
- ½ cup oil
- ½ cup honey
- 1 teaspoon vanilla

Preheat oven to 325°F. Grease an 8-inch square baking dish. Mix flour, wheat germ, baking powder and salt in large bowl. Stir in mixed fruit, chopped walnuts and sesame seeds.

In separate bowl, combine eggs, oil, honey and vanilla. Add to dry ingredients and stir lightly, just until blended. Spread in prepared dish and bake 35 to 40 minutes or until toothpick inserted in center comes out clean. Cool and cut into squares.

Fruit Sticks

Makes about 3 dozen

>   4 egg yolks
> ¼ cup light honey
>   2 teaspoons vanilla
> ¾ cup sifted whole wheat pastry flour
> ½ cup chopped walnuts
> ½ cup raisins
> ½ cup chopped apricots or dates

Preheat oven to 300°F. Line baking sheet with waxed paper; oil paper. Beat yolks in large bowl of electric mixer until foamy. Add honey and beat until frothy. Mix in vanilla. Fold in flour. Stir in walnuts, raisins and apricots.

Transfer mixture to pastry bag with ½- to ¾-inch opening (do *not* use pastry tube). Pipe out strips of dough to width of baking sheet, spacing about 4 inches apart. Bake 25 to 30 minutes. Cool on wire rack. Cut strips into 2-inch lengths. *Store sticks in airtight container.*

Congo Bars

Makes 32

½ cup plus 2 tablespoons (1¼ sticks) unsalted butter, room temperature

2⅓ cups firmly packed dark brown sugar

3 eggs

2½ cups unbleached all purpose flour

2 teaspoons baking powder

¼ teaspoon salt

1 12-ounce package semisweet chocolate chips

½ cup chopped walnuts

Preheat oven to 350°F. Grease 10 × 15-inch jelly roll pan. Beat butter with sugar in large bowl until light and creamy. Add eggs one at a time, beating well after each addition. Stir in flour, baking powder and salt and blend well. Fold in chips and nuts.

Turn into prepared pan, spreading evenly. Bake until top is lightly browned, about 20 to 25 minutes. Transfer to wire rack and cool. Cut into bars. *Store in airtight container.*

Congo Bars will freeze well.

Granola Bars

Makes about 2½ dozen

> ¾ cup butter or margarine, melted
> ⅓ cup firmly packed brown sugar
> ⅓ cup honey
> 1 teaspoon vanilla
> ½ teaspoon salt
> 4 cups granola
> ⅓ cup shelled sunflower seeds
> ⅓ cup chopped walnuts

Preheat oven to 400°F. Generously grease 10 × 15 × 1-inch baking pan. Combine butter, sugar and honey in large mixing bowl and blend well. Add vanilla and salt and beat until smooth. Stir in granola, seeds and nuts and mix thoroughly. Turn into prepared pan, spreading evenly to edges. Bake 15 to 18 minutes or until lightly browned. Cool completely and cut into squares. *Store in airtight container.*

Nutmeg Flats

Makes about 32

- 1 cup (2 sticks) unsalted butter, room temperature
- 1 cup sugar
- 1 egg yolk
- 2 cups unbleached all purpose flour
- 1½ teaspoons freshly grated nutmeg
- 1 egg white, beaten

Preheat oven to 275°F. Grease 10 × 15-inch jelly roll pan. Cream butter with sugar in large bowl until light and fluffy. Add egg yolk and beat well. Stir in flour and nutmeg, blending thoroughly. Turn into prepared pan, spreading evenly with fingertips. Brush top with beaten egg white. Bake until lightly browned, about 50 minutes. Cut into bars while still warm. *Store bars in airtight container.*

Grasshopper Bars

Makes about 40

   1½ cups sifted all purpose
         flour
    2 cups sugar
   ¾ cup plus 2 tablespoons
         instant cocoa mix
   1½ teaspoons salt
    1 teaspoon baking powder
   1⅓ cups butter
    4 eggs
    2 teaspoons vanilla
    2 tablespoons light corn
         syrup
    2 cups coarsely chopped
         toasted nuts

Mint Frosting
    2 cups sifted powdered
         sugar
   ¼ cup (½ stick) butter,
         softened
    2 tablespoons milk
    1 teaspoon mint extract
         Green food coloring

Chocolate Glaze
>   2 ounces unsweetened
>   chocolate
>   2 tablespoons butter

Icing for Wreaths
>   2 to 2½ tablespoons milk
>   ½ cup powdered sugar
>   Green food coloring

Preheat oven to 350°F. Sift first 5 ingredients into mixer bowl. Add butter, eggs, vanilla and corn syrup, mixing thoroughly. Fold in nuts. Spread batter in oiled 9 × 13 × 2-inch pan. Bake for 40 to 45 minutes, until soft in center and edges are slightly firm. Do not overbake. Cool.

Combine all ingredients for mint frosting, mixing thoroughly. Spread over cooled pastry. Place in freezer 15 to 20 minutes to harden. Cut pastry into 40 bars *but do not remove from pan.*

Heat chocolate and butter for chocolate glaze, blending thoroughly. When softened, brush evenly on top of mint frosting, using a pastry brush if desired. Allow chocolate to harden (refrigeration will speed the process). Carefully recut the bars. Remove from pan.

Add sufficient milk to powdered sugar to make firm icing for wreaths; mix until smooth. Stir in food coloring. Using a pastry bag and a small flower decorating tip, pipe a green wreath on each bar.

Store in tightly covered container, layered with sheets of waxed paper, or freeze.

Choco-Buttermilk Brownies

Makes about 32

　1　cup (2 sticks) unsalted butter, room temperature
　1　cup water
　5　tablespoons Dutch process cocoa

　2　cups sugar
　2　cups unbleached all purpose flour
　1　teaspoon salt
　½　cup buttermilk
　2　eggs
　1　teaspoon baking soda
　1　teaspoon vanilla

Icing

   ½ cup (1 stick) unsalted
      butter
   6 tablespoons buttermilk
   5 tablespoons Dutch
      process cocoa

   1 pound powdered sugar

      Chopped nuts (optional)

Preheat oven to 350°F. Generously grease 12 × 18-inch jelly roll pan. Melt butter in medium saucepan over medium heat. Stir in water and cocoa and whisk until smooth. Set aside.

Combine sugar, flour and salt in medium bowl. Add cocoa mixture, buttermilk, eggs, soda and vanilla and blend well. Pour into prepared pan. Bake until tester inserted in center comes out clean, 15 to 18 minutes.

For icing, melt butter in medium saucepan over medium heat. Add buttermilk and cocoa and whisk until smooth and creamy. Bring to boil.

Place powdered sugar in work bowl of processor or blender. With machine running, gradually add chocolate mixture, mixing until thick and smooth; do not overprocess.

Spread mixture generously over brownies. Sprinkle with nuts if desired. Refrigerate before cutting into squares. *Store in airtight container.*

Butterscotch Brownies

Makes about 2 dozen

- ½ cup (1 stick) butter
- 2 cups firmly packed dark brown sugar
- 2 teaspoons vanilla
- 2 eggs, lightly beaten
- 1 cup all purpose flour
- 2 teaspoons baking powder
- 1 teaspoon salt

Preheat oven to 350°F. Cream butter and brown sugar with electric mixer or in processor. Beat in vanilla and eggs. Sift together flour, baking powder and salt. Stir into creamed butter and brown sugar.

Butter a 9 × 13-inch baking pan. Add batter and spread evenly. Bake 35 to 40 minutes. *Do not overbake*. Cool completely before cutting into squares.

5

Small Pastries

Danish Elephant Ears

Makes 6 dozen

- 1 cup (2 sticks) unsalted butter
- 2 cups lightly packed all purpose flour
- 7 tablespoons ice water

- 1 cup sugar

In medium bowl cut butter into flour until dough resembles coarse meal. Gradually add water, stirring just until dough forms ball. Divide into 2 balls. Refrigerate 1 hour.

Grease baking sheets. Roll dough out to ¼-inch thickness and cut into 1½-inch rounds. Transfer to baking sheets and chill at least 30 minutes.

Preheat oven to 450°F. Dip rounds into sugar in shallow dish. Prick dough with fork. Bake until lightly browned, about 8 minutes, then turn and sprinkle again with sugar. Continue baking until sugar caramelizes, about 1 minute.

Scotch Shortbread

8 servings

- 1¼ cups all purpose flour
- ¼ cup sugar
- ½ cup (1 stick) butter, sliced, room temperature
- 3 tablespoons cornstarch
- 1 tablespoon sugar

Preheat oven to 375°F. Combine first 4 ingredients in medium bowl and blend until finely crumbled. Pat dough into 8- to 9-inch baking pan with removable bottom, spreading evenly. Press edges with tines of fork; gently prick bottom. Bake until lightly golden, about 25 minutes. Cool in pan 5 minutes. Cut

into wedges using sharp knife.
Sprinkle top with remaining
sugar. Let cool completely in pan
before serving, about 30 minutes.

Deluxe Baklava

Makes about 5 dozen

  2 pounds coarsely
     chopped walnuts
  1 pound coarsely chopped
     almonds
  ¾ cup sugar
  3 tablespoons cinnamon

  1 pound phyllo pastry
     sheets
  3 to 4 cups (6 to 8 sticks)
     unsalted butter, melted
1½ cups breadcrumbs, or
     mixture of breadcrumbs
     and vanilla wafer crumbs

     Syrup (see following
     recipe)

Place rack in center of oven and
preheat to 375°F. Grease 10 × 15-
inch baking pan; set aside.

Combine nuts, sugar and cinnamon in large mixing bowl.

Set aside 8 sheets of phyllo for top layer; cover with waxed paper and damp towel to prevent drying. Using remaining pastry, begin lining baking pan 1 sheet at a time, generously brushing each sheet with melted butter and sprinkling lightly with crumbs. Repeat until 8 sheets are used.

Sprinkle with layer of nut mixture, cover with another sheet of phyllo, brush with more butter and sprinkle with crumbs. Repeat layering until all nut mixture is used.

Place 1 reserved phyllo sheet over nuts. Brush with butter and sprinkle with crumbs. Repeat until all sheets are used. Brush top generously with butter.

Using sharp knife, preferably serrated, make 6 or 7 lengthwise cuts in baklava (number depends on size of pieces desired). Keep knife straight and make sure it slices through all layers. Use your free hand to gently hold phyllo behind knife.

After all lengthwise cuts are made, slice diagonally, beginning at upper corner of pan. Continue until all pastry has been cut into diamonds. Brush again with melted butter.

Bake 30 minutes, basting every 10 to 15 minutes. Reduce heat to 350°F and bake an additional 30 minutes or until golden, basting several times with butter that has accumulated on top. Cover loosely with aluminum foil if pastry browns too quickly.

While pastry is baking, prepare syrup (recipe below).

Toward end of baking time, test baklava for doneness by removing center piece. Pastry should be nicely browned and crisp. Spoon cooled syrup evenly over hot baklava. Cool completely in pan before removing pieces.

Syrup

- 4 cups sugar
- 2 cups water
- 1 slice fresh lemon, seeds removed
- 1 cinnamon stick

Combine all ingredients in medium saucepan and bring to boil over medium-high heat, stirring constantly until sugar is dissolved. Continue boiling gently, about 20 minutes. Remove from heat and allow to cool while baklava continues baking. Remove cinnamon stick before spooning over pastry.

Baklava may be wrapped individually in plastic wrap and stored in airtight container in refrigerator up to 2 months.

Jam-Filled Pastries (Puits d'Amour)

To ensure that these miniature patty shells all bake to a uniform height, place a rack over them held by 1½-inch-high heatproof supports in each corner.

Makes 2 dozen

> 2 pounds puff pastry
>
> 1 egg yolk
> 1 teaspoon water
>
> 1 cup raspberry jam or other flavor jam
> Powdered sugar

Lightly grease 2 baking sheets or line with parchment paper. Divide puff pastry dough evenly and roll each half to thickness of ⅛ inch. Transfer to prepared sheets in 1 piece, trimming off any excess. Chill 1 hour in coldest part of refrigerator or freeze for about 15 minutes.

Using 2½-inch-diameter sharp-edged cookie cutter, cut as many circles as possible from pastry, trimming excess as you work. Then, using 1¼-inch-diameter sharp-edged cookie cutter, cut center out of half the circles, leaving doughnut shape. Brush whole circles with water and place doughnut-shaped rings on top, pressing down lightly to secure. Chill 1 hour in coldest part of refrigerator or freeze for about 15 minutes.

Preheat oven to 400°F. Mix egg yolk with 1 teaspoon water. Brush shells with yolk mixture and bake until pastry is golden brown and has risen, about 15 minutes. Transfer to wire rack and cool completely. Fill each shell with jam and sprinkle with powdered sugar.

Pastries can be baked ahead of time and frozen. Recrisp 10 minutes in 350°F oven. Let cool completely before filling.

Petit Mont Blanc

These are tiny cheesecakes capped with chestnut puree.

Makes 4 dozen

   2 tablespoons unsalted butter
   3 tablespoons firmly packed light brown sugar
  ½ cup all purpose flour
  ¼ cup finely chopped walnuts or pecans

   8 ounces cream cheese, room temperature
  ¼ cup sugar
   1 egg
   2 tablespoons milk
   2 tablespoons fresh lemon juice
  ½ teaspoon vanilla

   1 15½-ounce can unsweetened chestnut puree

Preheat oven to 350°F. Cream butter; add brown sugar and flour, blending until mixture resembles cornmeal. Stir in nuts. Line miniature-size cupcake pan (cups should measure 1¾ inches wide by ⅞ inch deep) with paper bonbon liners. Press about ¾ teaspoon of nut mixture into bottom and slightly up the side of each liner. Bake for 10 minutes.

Beat together cream cheese and sugar. Beat in egg, milk, lemon juice and vanilla. Spoon into butter-nut mixture in cupcake cups. Bake 20 minutes or until cheese mixture has set. Cool.

Press chestnut puree through a ricer or coarse strainer onto tops of baked cakes (it will resemble vermicelli), or using a pastry bag and star tip, pipe a rosette of chestnut cream on top.

If wrapped carefully, these may be frozen for as long as 2 months.

6

Cookie Basics

These Basic Butter Cookies will make a nice addition to any baker's repertoire. The advantage of our buttery dough is that it is particularly easy to handle, so even children can share in making—and giving—something from the kitchen.

The dough can be flavored, shaped and decorated in a number of ways, from rolling chilled cylinders of it in cocoa or cinnamon to painting a batch with melted chocolate for a special glaze. We offer nearly a dozen exciting and tasty variations on the basic theme.

And as an added bonus, baked cookies freeze beautifully so an afternoon's work now will yield great dividends.

Equipment. Use shiny heavy aluminum baking sheets with low sides that won't deflect the heat. If only high-sided pans are available, turn them over and use the undersides. Although large sheets can hold more cookies, pans should ideally be at least two inches smaller than the oven rack on all sides to allow heat to circulate freely.

Timesaver. While the first batch of cookies bakes, shape, roll or cut uncooked dough as desired and arrange on lightly greased pieces of parchment paper or the shiny side of greased aluminum foil. Transfer paper to baking sheet. They will be all ready for the oven by the time the first batch is baked. Clean pan before reusing.

Basic Butter Cookies

Even cooking is the secret to success for all baked goods. If the last batch of cookies does not fill the baking sheet, invert a custard cup or small pan in any empty spaces to distribute the heat equally. If you suspect your oven has hot spots, turn the baking sheet around after five minutes in the oven.

Makes about 2½ dozen

- ½ cup (1 stick) unsalted butter, room temperature
- ½ cup sugar
- 2 egg yolks, room temperature
- 2 teaspoons vanilla
- 1 cup all purpose flour

Grease baking sheets. Cream butter with sugar in large bowl of electric mixer until fluffy. Beat in egg yolks and vanilla, stopping machine as necessary to scrape down sides of bowl. Add flour and continue beating just until mixed through; do not overbeat or cookies will be tough. Shape dough as desired (see below) and transfer to baking sheets. Chill before baking.

Position rack in center of oven and preheat to 350°F. Bake cookies *one sheet at a time* until edges are brown and centers are just firm to touch, about 8 to 10 minutes. Cool on racks.

Drop butter cookies: Using 2 spoons (one to push the batter off the other), drop dough by spoonfuls onto prepared baking sheet, spacing cookies 2 inches apart. Smooth and round cookies using knife (or your finger) dipped in cold water. For firmer cookies that will not spread very much, refrigerate dough for 30 minutes before baking.

Pressed butter cookies: Turn dough out onto plate, cover with plastic wrap and refrigerate for 1 hour, or until dough is firm enough to mold. Fill cookie press with dough and press out onto prepared baking sheet, spacing 1 inch apart. Or, spoon dough into damp pastry bag fitted with fluted tip (fill ⅔ full) and pipe out onto prepared sheet, spacing 1 inch apart. In both instances, return dough to refrigerator if it becomes too soft to mold. Refrigerate cookies 30 minutes before baking.

Rolled butter cookies: Flatten dough into rectangle ½ inch thick on sheet of waxed paper. Cover with another sheet of waxed paper. Refrigerate for 45 minutes or until firm. Without removing paper, roll dough out into rectangle ¼ inch thick. Return to refrigerator for 15 minutes. Discard top sheet of waxed paper. Using cookie cutter, knife or inverted beverage glass, cut as many shapes out of dough as possible. Arrange on prepared baking sheet, spacing 1 inch apart. Refrigerate 30 minutes. Meanwhile, gather scraps of dough into ball, reroll into rectangle, refrigerate and repeat rolling and cutting.

Refrigerator butter cookies: Turn dough out onto sheet of plastic wrap and, using plastic as aid, roll dough into cylinder 1 to 1½ inches thick. Wrap and refrigerate at least 12 hours. Slice into cookies ¼ inch wide and transfer to prepared baking sheet. (Dough can be prepared ahead and refrigerated up to 1 week.) If desired, roll cylinder in pearl (coarse) sugar, cocoa, cinnamon or chopped nuts before slicing and baking.

Filled butter cookies: To make a simple filled cookie, press thumb into formed cookie to make an indentation. Fill with jam, nuts, candy, chocolate chips, glacéed chestnuts, almond paste or dried or glacéed fruit. Or, put a very small amount of these ingredients in center of dough rounds and fold in half, pressing edges together firmly. Fillings can also be sandwiched between 2 formed cookies or spread on refrigerator butter cookie dough rolled ¼ inch thick. Roll dough out as for jelly roll and refrigerate. Then slice into pinwheels.

Decorating cookies: Cookies can be decorated before or after baking. To decorate before, paint on a design with melted chocolate or a colored egg wash, or roll in cinnamon, cocoa or tinted sugar. Paint with milk, cream or a lightly beaten egg white and top with coconut, silver dragées, chocolate or colored sprinkles, sesame or poppy seed, chopped nuts, or dried or candied fruit.

To decorate cookies after they are baked, roll in cocoa or powdered sugar or brush with egg white and roll in cinnamon, tinted sugar or coconut. Or, frost, cover with meringue and return briefly to a 500°F oven to brown. Cookies can also be glazed with powdered sugar that has been moistened with milk or cream. For a shiny surface, brush cookies lightly with warm corn syrup after baking.

Great Hints

- For soft chewy cookies allow less baking time; allow more time for crisp ones.
- Recrisp cookies by baking in 400°F oven for about 3 minutes.

- Glacéed fruit, pearl sugar, dipping chocolate and other quality baking supplies can often be purchased in quantity from a local baker or bakery supply.
- Use stiff cardboard to make cookie cutter patterns or stencils through which powdered sugar can be sifted.
- To avoid excessive browning, use solid vegetable shortening as opposed to butter or oil to grease baking sheets or foil.
- If dough becomes too soft to handle, refrigerate it briefly.
- If cookies are frosted or decorated, place a sheet of waxed paper between each layer before storing to prevent their sticking together.
- Package different cookies separately so they don't absorb other flavors.

Index

Credits

The following people contributed the recipes included in this book:

Sharon Cadwallader
Marion Gorman
Carolyn Hall
Jacki Horwitz
Beverly Jackson
Sharon Katz
Margaret H. Koehler
Judy Kostin
Rita Leinwand
Janine McGregor
Jinx and Jefferson Morgan
Lori Openden
Joyce Resnik
Sondra Rykoff
Susan Sandler
Jack Schneider
Ship Ahoy, Essex, Massachusetts
Barbara Tomorowitz
Susan Unterberg
Sheri Wayne
Jan Weimer
Rhoda Yee